WINTER
WONDERLAND COLORING BOOK

TERESA GOODRIDGE

DOVER PUBLICATIONS, INC.
MINEOLA, NEW YORK

The winter season brings joy and ethereal beauty to the world. This gallery of winter scenes depicts pristine snow-covered villages, panoramic landscapes, and eager children bundled up in scarves and gloves building a snowman and window-shopping at a toy store. This charming collection also includes images of fun winter sports such as skiing, ice skating on frozen ponds, and riding in a horse-drawn sled. Specially designed for the experienced colorist, the illustrations in this book will keep you warm and cozy while you experiment with color and different media. Each of the thirty-one plates has been perforated for removal to make displaying your work easy.

Copyright
Copyright © 2016 by Dover Publications, Inc.
All rights reserved.

Bibliographical Note
Winter Wonderland Coloring Book is a new work, first published by
Dover Publications, Inc., in 2016.

International Standard Book Number
ISBN-13: 978-0-486-80501-6
ISBN-10: 0-486-80501-8

Manufactured in the United States by LSC Communications
80501810   2019
www.doverpublications.com